City Rocks
City Blocks
and the Moon

by Edward Gallob
Photographs by the author

Edward Gallob

St Peters School
11/74

City Rocks
City Blocks
and the Moon

CHARLES SCRIBNER'S SONS
NEW YORK

For Jeneva and Jachin

1 3 5 7 9 11 13 15 17 19 RD/C 20 18 16 14 12 10 8 6 4 2

Printed in the United States of America
Library of Congress Catalog Card Number 73-1333
SBN 684-13542-6

Contents

Geology Is...

This book is about the adventure you can have as a geologist in the city.

Geology is people, plants and animals living together on this earth. Geology is mountains and tall buildings, muddy city rivers, and rain water running down a city street; dust storms, and the wind blowing sand and leaves across a city park.

Geology is looking for fossils in old rocks as a record of ancient life, or your dog's footprints in today's wet-cement sidewalk.

Magnified coral fossil in shale

Geology is the changing earth—mountains becoming hills, becoming plains, becoming a valley with a stream. Sea shells becoming limestone, becoming marble.

Geology is trees pushing up and breaking pavements and an
iron fence rusting away.

The pebbles you pick up and throw, the one you keep for its pattern or the luck it will bring, or just because it feels good in your hand.

Geology is finding mica or garnet crystals in the walls of your school building.

Walking barefoot and feeling wet mud between your toes.

Magnified garnet crystals

If you live in the city you may have thought of going off to some mountain or quarry to hunt rocks or fossils. Or perhaps you have thought of rocketing to the moon, bringing back its rocks to solve the mysteries of the moon. But, in fact, a geologic adventure with the earth is at your city doorstep.

Rocks and fossils are all around us in the city.

The granite curbstone.

The limestone with ancient fossils from the sea.

The white marble steps you sit on.
The sandy brownstones that cover the front of your house.

The planet earth is a huge rock. Together with a great variety of plants and animals, we live on a thin layer of sand, soil, broken rock and large areas of surface water. Sometimes we have to dig deep to find it, but solid bedrock is always there under the land and sea. And sometimes we find outcroppings of firm bedrock without having to dig at all.

Rocks are different from each other, and yet they are alike in many ways. All rocks have minerals, color, texture, hardness, size and shape. These features give each rock a certain look, or pattern, that suggests their environment at the time they were formed.

Perhaps there were volcanoes spreading flows of lava. Frost and rain wearing away hills and mountains. Glaciers, rivers and

the wind moving the worn parts of the earth and settling them in new places. The ever-moving earth, sometimes suddenly, or over long periods of time, rising, stretching, twisting, squeezing, changing its rocks and minerals. Every rock is a resting place in time, a part of the geologic history of the earth.

Prehistoric American Indians left no written record of their homes, their food or clothing, yet archeologists—by using the excavated artifacts and features of the dig—have put together a picture story of their times and how they lived.

In the same way, the geologist—who was not present when rocks were formed—uses the patterns of the rocks to try to put together the story of their formation. Using these patterns of the past, geologists divide the earth's rocks into three broad groups: igneous, sedimentary and metamorphic.

Igneous Rock

The paving block of your street, the tough curbstone at the edge of your cement pavement is very probably an igneous rock formed millions of years ago when the earth—originally in a molten state—cooled and hardened.

Have you ever thought of digging a deep hole that would go all the way to China? Have you ever wondered what you would find on the way down? No one really knows, but you could think about it.

Geologists know that it is very hot deep inside the earth, and they believe that the rocks and minerals there may be in a molten state. No one knows exactly why, but from time to time a molten material called magma works its way toward the earth's surface as lava to form two types of rocks, known as basalt and granite.

Granite

Granite is the most familiar city rock. It has a coarse-grained pattern and large interlocking crystals. Its salt and pepper pattern is usually light gray, but it can be pink or reddish.

Hard and tough, it is used at the bottom of large buildings, as curbstones, cobblestones, and paving blocks, and generally in areas that take great wear. In construction built to last for a long time, solid blocks of granite are placed one on the other, as in the Egyptian pyramids.

Smooth granite, beautiful and majestic, is found in monuments and statues.

Granite is mainly composed of feldspar and quartz, the most abundant minerals in the earth's crust. The satin smooth spots in granite are feldspar, and the glassy spots are quartz. The dark flecks are mica crystals.

Basalt

Basalt is a form of igneous rock created from magma that came to the earth's surface and spread out in huge flows of lava. On exposure to air, it cooled quickly forming fine-grained rock with very small mineral crystals.

If you live in Hawaii, you are on a solid island of basalt. Most of the earth's crust under the ocean and many of its volcanic islands are basalt. Dark, dense and massive, it is easy to recognize as the huge, irregular jetty stones in the river and harbor, dark curb and paving stone, building stone in old Gothic churches, or the small ballast stones that hold railroad tracks in place. Traprock is a common name for basalt and similar dark, fine-grained rocks. The Palisades across the Hudson River from New York City are cliffs of traprock.

Rocks, as with most other things in nature, are seldom exactly one thing or the other. As a red rose is sometimes a little yellow or a little blue, so granite and basalt in varying amounts make up a group of other rocks with in-between colors and textures, and with names like rhyolite, andesite, diorite, gabbro and diabase.

21

Sedimentary Rock

The Effect of Change

Sedimentary rocks are formed from the broken-down weathered parts of other rocks. Weathering is the change that takes place in rocks that are exposed to the atmosphere, water, plant and animal life, including of course, people. Without weathering, the earth's landscape might be as the moon—its original igneous rocks unchanged.

The weathering action of lichens on bare rock loosens the rock's particles, which, together with the decayed lichens, become pockets of soil for mosses, followed by grasses, ferns and small plants.

Rain and frost eroding words from gravestones.

Gravity pulling stones from walls and cliffs.

Summer heat softening, winter ice expanding asphalt streets.

The river flooding, depositing mud on your doorstep.

Waves pounding rocks on the beach and stones in the jetties.

The beginning of a sedimentary rock may be in the bits of
sandy soil carried by rain water along the street curbs,
or canyons of sand cut by running water in the park.

After a heavy rain, your city's river is colored by mud, sand
and gravel washed from miles of its banks.

Eventually, the river (at times overflowing and leaving
plains of mud) will reach a lake or ocean where its sediments,
sorted by the waters, will settle out in their own places.
Where the river slows down, its heavier and coarser-grained
particles will drop first to form conglomerate rocks. Then
medium-grained sands will settle to become sandstones. Where
the waters are quietest, finer sands and clays join together
as mudstone and shale.

Sandstone

    If you live in an eastern city, there may be houses in your neighborhood called brownstones. These homes are made of brick and covered with brown sandstone. Sandstone is made of rounded grains of sand pressed and cemented together. It has a gritty feeling, and if you scrape it with a harder stone, grains of sand will come off. It can be a dull yellow, white, red or brown. Sometimes it has layers of different-colored sand running through it.

Limestone

Limestone is a light-colored building stone that resembles
sandstone, but if you look closely you may discover small
sea shells in its surface. Or you may see that the stone is
all shell fragments.

Limestone is the accumulation of the shells and skeletons
of sea life, both animal and plant, that died and settled in
the water. Over a long period of time, thick layered deposits of
these limy materials build up and harden into limestone.

Shellfish build their protective shells by extracting the mineral
calcite from the waters in which they live. Calcite is also
the cementing agent in sandy sedimentary rocks. Sometimes
calcite will precipitate from sea water to become a
crystallized form of limestone.

Shale and Mudstone

Shale and mudstones are the most abundant of the exposed sedimentary rocks. Shale is mostly hardened clay and smells like mud when wet.

Shale is formed when sediment is deposited in thin layers by water over a period of time—between high tides or periodic floodings. Look for what will some day be shale in quiet water areas, muddy lakes and flooded banks. Most shales crumble easily, but those with more sand harden to form massive mudstones called agrilites.

Shale

31

Sand

A grain of sand is a worn-down rock.

Sands and pebbles used in building are mostly quartz.
Quartz is one of the most common minerals on the earth's
surface. It is hard and weather resistant. However, sands can
be any of the other rock-forming minerals, or a combination
of them.

For example, there is white calcite from limestone, colored
clays from feldspars, sparkling mica, dark minerals from
basalt and sometimes reddish garnet sands.

The sands you find deposited by rain and running water
will vary from place to place, according to the nature of the
weathered rocks the water passed through. The rocks may
be nearby or many miles upstream.

Coal

In the city ferns grow in clay pots. Millions of years ago
they grew and died, together with giant mosses, rushes
and scaly trees in dense swampy forests. Season after season
their abundant dead parts piled up into thick layers of
spongy peat.

In time the swampy forests were covered with muddy
sediments that hardened to layers of shale, sandstone and
limestone. The great pressure of these rocks—together
with heat—over millions of years changed the soft peat into coal.

Plant fossils can be found in the layered rocks above the
coal, but not in the hard coal itself.

Fossils

A fossil is the remains of, or the impression made by, animals or plants that lived in the past. The "past" can be yesterday, or a million years ago.

You can discover in the field or the museum bones of prehistoric animals, shells of ancient sea creatures, impressions of insects and plants in stone, the trails left by crawling snails and worms, or the footprints of a dinosaur.

Most fossils are of plants and animals that lived in or came to wet places leaving their remains or impression in soft sediments that hardened. The sedimentary rocks—shales, sandstone and limestone—are good fossil-hunting places.

The city has its own fossil places—muddy playgrounds, soft asphalt streets and wet-concrete pavements.

34

Metamorphic Rock

Most of nature responds to a new environment by changing its form. As you know, water becomes ice when it is cold and steam when hot. Soft clay pressed and heated becomes a hard brick.

When the environment of a rock changes, the rock changes. All or some of its features (minerals, color, texture, hardness, size and shape) will change in response to the new environment.

The change may be slight or so great that the identity of the original rock is lost. Marble, quartzite, slate, schist and gneiss are all forms of metamorphic rock created through changing conditions below the earth's surface that we can only guess at.

Perhaps there was great heat from volcanic action that softened the rocks, thus allowing change, or the pressure of mountain-forming movements, or the flow of lava, gases or liquids that invaded the rocks, changing or exchanging their minerals.

Marble

The marble statues of men and horses, the polished marble slabs covering walls, and the hard marble steps of the building where you live were once limestone, now changed into this new rock with larger crystals.

Although pure marble is white, some marble is colored, or has streaked patterns of color that come from the mineral, plant or animal matter in the original limestone.

All limy materials—marble, limestone and sea shells—will bubble and fizz to a drop of dilute hydrochloric acid or very strong vinegar.

Quartzite

The common light brown pebble found in gravel is the metamorphic rock quartzite. It is a sandstone whose small sandy crystals have been changed by heat and pressure and are now larger and fused together, forming one of the hardest, toughest and most stable rocks.

Quartzite will not split into smooth thin layers like slate, or break around its grain as sandstone does. It fractures through the quartz grains into pieces with sharp edges with a random surface and a glossy luster.

Protect your eyes with goggles or place the pebbles in a bag before breaking them.

Slate

In the early days, before cement sidewalks and painted blackboards, large slabs of slate were used as pavements and as school blackboards. Many are still around. Slate comes from the sedimentary rock shale, whose soft layers break into oddly-shaped flakes. Slate—flattened and hardened by great heat and pressure—splits easily into thin slabs.

Schist

The shiny building stone with mica flakes or garnet is a
mica-schist. Schists break in their own special way, with a wavy
uneven surface forming irregularly shaped rocks with
ragged edges. Thick wavy layers of cement mortar hold the
stones together. Mica-schist was once a shale or mudstone, now
changed by great heat and pressure. Its mica crystals, which
are broad and flat, are all facing one direction like a pile
of autumn leaves.

Gneiss (pronounced "nice")

Gneisses are metamorphic rocks that have undergone great change. Their individual minerals, once separate in the granites and sedimentary rocks, have come together in parallel streaks or alternating dark and light layers that may become stretched, flattened, twisted, or even folded.

When stonemasons were plentiful, these abundant rocks were used as building stones. Today as crushed stone they cover countless parking lots and fill the shoulders of miles of highway.

Man-made Rocks

Even man-made rocks come from the earth—bricks from clay, cement sidewalks from the shells and mud of the sea, and glass from quartz rocks.

Since the time when clay objects were baked in the sun or hardened in a hearth, man has been molding and firing clay into bricks, pottery, tiles and pipes.

Sometimes it is difficult to tell a man-made rock from one made by nature. Cement walls can look like limestone. Concrete pavements are—as is sedimentary rock—a mixture of water, sand, gravel and crushed rock, held together by cement.

Cement is mostly finely ground limestone and shale, burned to a glassy clinker which then is reground to become cement. Mixed with water it hardens to become a man-made rock.

Glass is like the volcanic rock obsidian which is formed when molten lava cools rapidly. It is made by melting mostly quartz rocks with other minerals and then cooling them so rapidly that they do not crystallize, thereby remaining translucent.

And Now the Moon

Man has landed on the moon. The astronauts have returned again and again, bringing back "moon rocks" to help answer one of man's oldest questions: what is the moon made of?

The moon rocks are volcanic in origin, resembling the earth's fine-grained basalts. Although billions of years old, they are unchanged except for the impact of meteorites that pulverized the original moon rocks into the minute fragments that make up the soil of the lunar surface. In addition to the shattering effect of the meteorites, the tremendous heat and pressure of their impact fused the minute fragments, forming breccia rocks.

A breccia is a rock made up of fragments which are rough and angular, showing little or no sign of wear or travel. It is as if they were joined together close to the place where they were formed.

A conglomerate is a rock made up of well-rounded fragments worn smooth by the tumbling action of fast water. There are no conglomerates on the moon.

From our observation and understanding of our own atmosphere and its weathering effect on the earth, we conclude, in studying the moon rocks, that the moon never formed an atmosphere.

Lacking an atmosphere, the moon has been without weather, without moisture to capture the sun's heat or to evaporate as clouds; without rain, snow, dew and frost; without ponds, rivers, lakes and oceans; without plant and animal life.

Without all these, the rocks never eroded, never were split by frost, worn by rain, polished by the wind, and never carried by running water to new places to become new rocks.

The moon's environment remained the same, unchanged except for wandering meteors and the very recent footsteps of man.

What if a spaceship from outer space landed in your school yard and its astronauts said to you, "Will you help us collect the 'earth rocks' in your area that would tell us about the earth and the conditions that existed when these rocks were formed?"

What would you collect?

Collecting

Collecting is bringing back your bit of the earth.

Collecting should be fun. There are no rules of what to collect, where to keep, or how to label your collection. Being a rock hound is doing your thing with the earth. Collect any part of the earth that pleases you.

Some fishermen bring back only a story; some stamp collectors try for one from every country.

You may enjoy poking around empty lots for the remaining stones of old buildings, walking through roads cut from solid rock, turning mounds of excavated earth, finding pebbles along the water's edge.

On an exposed ledge of bedrock you may discover a crystal of red garnet, clear mica, black hornblende, a fossil, or a blue lichen.

Perhaps a rocky ledge of your own—never to take—but a place to come back to.

Index

References to photographs are printed in boldface type.